KU-078-551

Contents

Any words appearing in the text in bold, **like this**, are explained in the glossary.

This is Spain

Spain is a large country in south-western Europe. In the north, there are many high mountains. In the centre of the country there is a huge, dry **plateau**, called the *Meseta*. This is the Spanish word for 'plateau'. Along the south coast there are sandy beaches.

Seville is a major city in south-western Spain. This is a view of the city at night.

The Canary Islands lie off the coast of Africa, but they are a part of Spain. Many tourists visit the Canary Islands' beaches.

Spain has many interesting cities. Two of the largest are Madrid, the capital, and Barcelona. Seville, in the south-west, has a famous building called the Tower of Gold. Its name comes from the golden tiles that covered the walls around the city. Valencia is a port on the Mediterranean Sea.

Spain also has beautiful countryside. There you can see orange and olive trees growing.

This book will show you some of these places. It will also tell you much about the country of Spain. If you learn about Spain before you take your camera there, you will enjoy your visit more.

The place

Spain is the third largest country in Europe. It is almost square in shape. The country is about 950 kilometres (590 miles) from north to south and about 1085 kilometres (675 miles) from east to west. Spain is over twice the size of the United Kingdom.

The Atlantic Ocean is on the north-western side of Spain. The Mediterranean Sea is on the south-eastern side. The Pyrénées mountains in the north-east divide Spain and France. These mountains are about 450 kilometres (280 miles) long. Spain has more mountains than any other country in Europe except Switzerland.

Portugal borders Spain in the west. Together Spain and Portugal make up the Iberian Peninsula. A peninsula is a piece of land surrounded on three sides by water.

Two groups of islands belong to Spain. One is the Balearics, which is made up of five islands. They are in the Mediterranean Sea. The other group of islands is the Canary Islands. They are in the Atlantic Ocean, very close to Africa. The Canary Islands are made up of seven islands.

FRANCE

ANDORRA

Santander

•Pamplona

P y r é n é e s

E b r o   R i v e r

Barcelona
•

PORTUGAL

Madrid
✪

Balearic
Sea

M e s e t a

T a g u s   R i v e r

Valencia•

Balearic
Islands

I b e r i a n   P e n i n s u l a

Mediterranean Sea

•Seville

N

100 km

0   100 Miles

Strait of Gibraltar

MOROCCO

7

**The Pyrénées Mountains are in north-eastern Spain. They rise
to a height of 3404 metres (11,168 feet).**

Gibraltar is a small piece of land in the south. It is
just 6.5 square kilometres (3 square miles) in size and
only 13 kilometres (8 miles) wide at its narrowest
point.

Much of the land that faces the Atlantic Ocean is
covered with forests. This is a moutainous region where
few people live. Along the Mediterranean Sea there are
many sandy beaches and holiday resorts. This part of
Spain includes the popular beaches of the *Costa del Sol*,
which means 'Coast of the Sun'.

The weather in northern Spain is cooler and wetter than in the south. There is usually rain in the winter and sometimes in the summer. Along the Mediterranean Sea the climate is warm and sunny for much of the year.

Spain's longest river is the Tagus. The river runs through both Spain and Portugual. In Spanish its name is *Tajo*. Spain's second longest river is the Ebro, which flows into the Mediterranean Sea. All of Spain's other main rivers flow into the Atlantic Ocean.

Gibraltar is on the Mediterranean Sea. It is a part of the Iberian Peninsula, although its residents speak English.

Madrid

Madrid became the capital of Spain in 1561. The city was chosen because it is in the centre of the country, in the region of Castile.

Madrid sits on a **plateau** that is 640 metres high. The city has very hot summers and cold winters. Most days are sunny, which allow the people of Madrid to enjoy outdoor cafés and restaurants.

Madrid is a modern city. More than 4 million people live there. The city has broad avenues lined with modern office blocks and many old buildings, too. One of them is the Royal Palace, built in the 18th century. It has 2800 rooms, which makes it one of the world's largest palaces. Today the Royal Palace is a museum.

Madrid is also the home of one of the world's largest art museums, the Prado, and the city also has a famous flea market, called the Rastro.

Spanish TV, newspapers and many international companies are based in Madrid. Recently the clothing, leather and fashion **industries** have become very important in Madrid.

Because Madrid is in the centre of the country, it has become the country's major railway hub.

If you took your camera around the streets of Madrid, you could photograph all sorts of sights.

This is Plaza Mayor, which is right in the centre of Madrid. It was built in the 17th century.

Places to visit

Spain has many amazing places to visit, both in the towns and in the countryside.

The Alhambra is a palace and fort in Granada in the south of the country. These buildings were constructed by the Moors, people from North Africa who conquered Spain in CE 711. Moorish kings lived in the Alhambra for more than 200 years.

Barcelona is the second largest city in Spain. It is one of the country's main ports. Antonio Gaudí, a famous architect, lived in Barcelona. His best known work is the Church of the Sagrada Familia in Barcelona. This means 'holy family' in English. The **cathedral** was begun in 1884, but it still has not been finished.

Spain has about 10,000 caves in its mountain areas. The Altamira caves, near the city of Santander in the north, are world famous. In 1879 a young girl went to the caves with her father. Inside the caves she noticed paintings of animals that experts think are about 15,000 years old.

The Alhambra has beautiful stone carvings that are so fine, they look like lace.

The people

More than 40 million people live in Spain. About 5000 years ago, a people known as Iberians lived there. Over time, groups of people from other parts of Europe came to Spain. More than 1200 years ago, Moors came from North Africa.

The official language of Spain is a type of Spanish called Castilian, but people in different parts of the country pronounce the words differently. Many places in Spain

A quarter of Spanish people are under the age of sixteen.

The Spanish can always find time to meet and talk news or politics with their friends.

have their own language as well as Castilian Spanish. In the area of Catalonia, many people speak Catalan. This is similar to the language spoken by people of southern France. Catalan Spanish is spoken in Barcelona.

In the **Basque** area, some people speak their own language. Basque is one of the oldest languages in Europe. It is not like any other language in the world. Basques were living in the mountains of northern Spain long before Spain became a country.

Life in Spain

Almost half of the population of Spain lives on about 15 per cent of the land. Many people are moving from the country to the cities to look for work. They are also moving to holiday resorts on the south coast for the same reason. Most of the people who move to the cities are young.

People often dance a well-known Spanish dance called the flamenco during special festivals.

In some parts of Spain, people still get around on mules.

The family is at the centre of Spanish life. Until recently, many mothers did not work. They stayed at home to take care of their children. Now families are smaller, and many mothers get a job to help earn money. Even so, fewer women in Spain work than in most other European countries.

In Spain, dinner often does not begin until 9:30 or 10:00 p.m. This is because much of Spain is hot. People take a long break, or *siesta*, during the hottest part of the day. Then they go back to work around 5:00 p.m. Sometimes, in the evenings, when the weather has cooled down, people in the cities take a walk along the main streets or in the squares before dinner. This walk is known as the *paseo*.

17

Government and religion

Spain is a **parliamentary** monarchy. This means that a monarch (king or queen) is the head of state. However, it is parliament that makes the laws. The parliament is called the Cortes and it is made up of the Congress of Deputies and the Senate. The head of the Cortes is the prime minister. The citizens of Spain elect their representatives to the Cortes for four years.

Most Spanish people are **Roman Catholics**. A few **Muslims**, **Protestants** and **Jews** live in Spain, but there are not very many. The second-largest **cathedral** in the world is in Spain. Called Santa Maria, it is in Seville. It was built between 1402 and 1506. The church is 125.8 metres long and 82 metres wide.

Spain has many fine churches and cathedrals. This is the Cathedral of Santiago de Compostela in Santiago.

18

Earning a living

The biggest **industry** in Spain is tourism. More than 50 million visitors a year come to Spain to enjoy the country's warm weather and sandy beaches. Tourism now employs 60 per cent of Spain's work force.

About a third of Spain's workers are employed in manufacturing, making cars, electrical goods, clothing

Because Spain is surrounded by so much water, fishing is an important industry.

and textiles, heavy machinery, toys, steel and food and drink. Spain has few **natural resources** apart from **fossil fuels** and minerals. Coal and **iron ore** are found in the north. Most raw materials, including oil, are bought, or imported, into Spain.

Farming takes place across Spain, but especially in the north, where sheep, cows and goats are raised. Farmers grow cereal crops such as wheat and barley in the Meseta. In the warm south, farmers grow fruits and vegetables. Grapes that are made into wine are also grown in Spain. Olives are another important food crop. Some of the olives are **exported**. Many are made into olive oil.

People cut down too many trees in the past, but this has now largely stopped. Many new trees have been planted in the last 20 years. Now Spain has more hectares of forest than any other country in Europe. Especially important are the cork oak trees. The bark from these trees is made into bottle stoppers and pin boards.

Spain has one of the world's largest fishing fleets. These fish for tuna in the Mediterranean and cod and other fish in the Atlantic Ocean.

Schools and sport

In Spain, children start school when they are six years old. The school day starts early and finishes late. Students take a break during the middle of the day, when it is very hot. At the age of sixteen, students who pass an exam can begin studying for a place at university. Some universities in Spain are more than 800 years old. The University of Madrid has more than 100,000 students.

Football is Spain's most popular team sport. The national team and some of its football clubs are among the best in the world.

Pelota is a fast-moving **Basque** ball game, played on an indoor court. Cycling, hiking, swimming and diving are also popular sports.

Bullfighting is a famous Spanish sport. Bullfights are called *corridas*. Many people around the world dislike these events because of the cruelty shown to the animals. Despite this, bullfights are still popular in Spain.

In Spain, football is known by its Spanish name, *fútbol*.

food and festivals

Spain is famous for its fish and seafood dishes. Spanish people eat at least twice as much fish each year as most other Europeans. Other popular foods are sausages, ham and cheese.

One of Spain's most popular dishes is *paella*. This is a kind of stew made of fish, seafood, meat and rice in a rich broth. Meals may be finished with *flan*, a cooked custard, or with locally grown fruit.

Because most Spanish people are **Roman Catholics**, most festivals are religious ones. One of the best known is Holy Week. It is called *Semana Santa* in Spanish. This is the week before Easter. During this time, there are many religious parades.

Some Spanish festivals, or *fiestas*, may last as long as a week. Many Spanish people celebrate harvests with parades. These usually take place in October. In Pamplona, a city in northern Spain, there is a *fiesta* in which bulls are allowed to run through the streets.

24

A tomato festival.

Christmas in Valencia.

The future

When you go to Spain, you will see a country that is changing. Many new things are happening there. Today, electronics, chemicals and computers are important **industries**. They bring money into the country. They also create jobs for many people.

However, like other nations, Spain has some problems. Many of the roads in Spain are new and large. One in four Spanish people own cars. This means there is a lot of traffic. This is especially true in the summer, when tourists crowd the roads.

In Spain, there has been some damage to the **environment**. This has happened mainly in the cities and tourist resorts. Many national parks have been set up to protect animals and plants.

The Spanish are proud of their country. When you leave Spain, a Spanish person might say 'Hasta la vista' to you. This is Spanish for 'See you later'.

Many tourists come to the Costa del Sol. This helps the Spanish economy, but damages the coastline.

26

Quick facts about
SPAIN

Capital
Madrid

Borders
France, Gibraltar, Portugal

Area
504,750 sq km
(194,884 square miles)

Population
40 million

Largest cities
Madrid (4,072,000 people);
Barcelona (2,819,000 people);
Valencia (754,000 people)

Main crops
grains, vegetables, olives, grapes,
sugar beet, citrus fruits, beef, pork,
poultry, dairy products, fish

Natural resources
coal, lignite, iron ore, uranium,
mercury

Longest river
Tajo, at 1007 km (626 miles)

Flag of Spain

Coastline
4964 km (3085 miles)

Monetary unit
euro

Literacy rate
98 per cent of Spanish people can read and write.

Major industries
machinery, metals, textiles, shoes, vehicles, processed food, tourism

29

Glossary

Basques (BASKS) people based in the Pyrénées mountains, on the borders of Spain and France, whose language is unlike Spanish or French

cathedral main church, where the bishop of an area is based

environment natural surroundings

export when products are sold to another country

fossil fuel fuel that comes from the remains of ancient living organisms

industry making goods and products

iron ore rock that contains iron deposits

Jew (JOO) follower of Judaism, a religion that worships one God, and that awaits the coming of God's chosen one, or Messiah

Muslim (MUHZ-luhm) person who follows the teachings of the prophet Mohammed and the religion he founded in the 7th century CE, Islam

natural resources things from nature that are useful to people

Parliament group of people who are elected to make the laws

plateau (PLA-toe) flat area of land that is higher than the land around it

Protestant those Christian churches that broke away from the Catholic Church in the 16th century. Protestants believe that God can be reached less through church authorities and more through personal faith and Bible studies.

Roman Catholic Christian church, based in Rome, Italy, that considers the Pope to be Christ's representative on Earth.

Index